The Art

Small Talk

Master the Unwritten Code of Social Skills,
Talk to Anyone, Improve Your Charisma, and
Make Real Friends Effortlessly

Mark Anderson

First Published: May 2021

Table of Contents

Your Free Gift

Discover the Strategies to Rule the Art of Conversation!

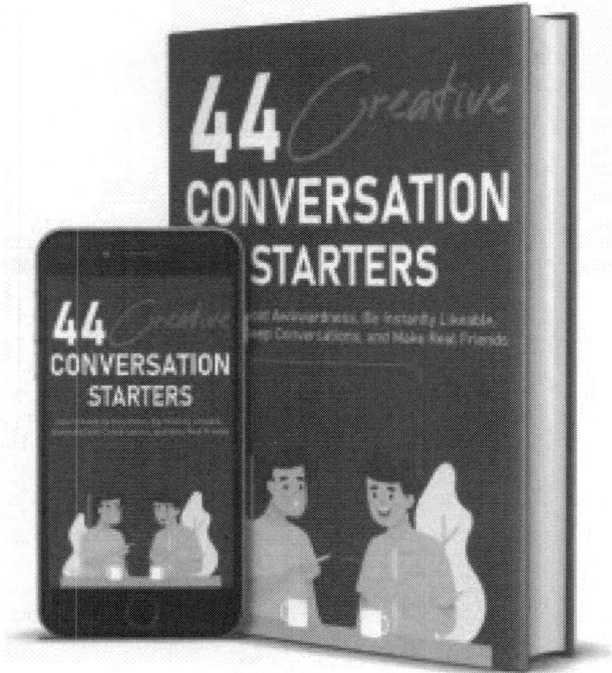

You'll learn how to how to avoid awkwardness, be instantly likeable, generate deep conversations, and make real friends.

You can get this free copy by providing your email address.

In this book you will find:
- Conversation starters for any situation
- Take your conversation to a deeper level

- How to have off-the-wall conversation
- Conversations for work appropriate topics

To get your bonus go to:

www.prolifemastery.com/conversation/

Introduction

Life as a shy and introverted person puts you in a very narrow box. Your experiences in life are limited to you and the things that happen around you; which let's face it, might not be much. 2020 gave us a global pandemic that thrust the world into isolation and for many introverts, it sounded like the perfect situation for everyone. Until you realize that we need people and relationships with people to thrive. However, just because we have a fundamental need to be around people does not mean we should entertain negative and toxic people as a part of our bonding journey. It is possible to be an introvert and still have healthy relationships with people. After everything the world has been through lately, his new year is like a reset button. As we begin reentry into the new "normal", many people have had to learn to socialize again.

Seize this new transitional period as your opportunity to reclaim your place in society. Most introverts live their lives as outcasts in society. They do not get invited to social events and even when they do get an invite, they are left on the sidelines. This doesn't have to be the case anymore. You can change your story, step into the spotlight and reclaim your shine. It is okay to love yourself and enjoy your company however if this is getting in the way of your ability to navigate through social situations even the basic ones that are essential for you it is time to switch things up and get the best out of every relationship that you get into. Because while being a loner has its moments, eventually, it can cause you to miss out on some of life's most amazing adventures and opportunities.

I remember reading somewhere that your net worth is determined by your network. In other words, it is the people that you know that will determine how much you are worth and I'm not talking about hard currency or physical wealth. Although your network can also contribute to this, I am talking about the wealth of experiences that you accrue over time. But having the right network is not going to simply fall on your laps. People are not going to be lining up at the door to become your friends or a part of your social circle. You are the one who needs to put in the work to get that to happen. For a standard introvert, the thought of getting out there to mingle and make friends can be scary. For anyone determined to turn their life around for the better, all they need is to take the first step. This is where this book, *"The Art of Small"* comes in.

In this book, you would learn the unique features you possess that make you, you, and how you can play that into any conversation or social situation to make friends. In addition to this you will also discover;

- Effective confidence building techniques
- How to strike engaging conversations in a romantic situation
- A practical guide to reinventing yourself socially
- Public speaking tips that would leave your audience in the palm of your hands
- How to negotiate any deal in your favor

If you are tired of living in the shadows and are ready to get out there and be the best version of yourself, you can turn it over to the next page. Please note; only do this if you are absolutely ready to begin the most adventurous part of your journey in life. I look forward to seeing you on the other side.

Chapter One

Fundamental Facts About Shyness

The society that we live in today is made up of a lot of labels. Each of these labels has unique traits through which people identify themselves. Shyness is a trait largely associated with people who are under the label of introverts. But when you explore shyness in-depth, you would be surprised to discover that there are extroverts who are shy. Does this mean that shyness is good? Or is it bad? Is this another social label and does it have any negative impact on your relationship experiences? This is what we are going to find out in this chapter.

The Science Behind Shyness

To get to the root of any problem, you have to start at the very beginning. With a touchy subject like this, the starting point is usually our genes. You want to know what part we inherited from our parents or socially reclusive ancestors. If your suspicions turn out to be true, perhaps science can explain this weird phenomenon to us. After reaching a hypothesis like this, the next step is to ask questions. Is it possible that your inability to socialize or connect with people in a public setting is directly linked to your DNA? Are you genetically programmed to be shy? I wish I had a long dramatic response that would explain why you act the way you do. But the long and short of everything is that your shyness can only be 30% attributed to your DNA. The rest is down to your environment and your social experiences growing up.

I had mixed feelings when I first found out about this data. For one thing, I was expecting DNA to be completely responsible for my extreme shyness. It would make it easier to just push it down to my genes and leave things at that because you can't change your DNA. Once it's fixed in your DNA, it's fixed. However, this bit of news tore that logic down to shreds and placed the reason for my shyness squarely on my upbringing and my environment. When you think of the statistics numerically, 30% is a lot. But in the larger scheme of things, it doesn't hold the controlling majority of the responsibility for how you act in social situations. Life is so much easier when someone else is responsible for your woes. Knowing that your shyness is something that is within your control can be daunting at the very least. But that is only because of the perspective you have right now. If you look at things from the other side of the glass, it means that you can take charge and change the narrative if you want.

So what is the point of this segment, you wonder. I wanted to show you that your current condition, as difficult as it is, does not require someone with an outstanding medical degree to cure it. There is also no need to participate in some experimental drug program to become more confident. The key to letting go of your shyness and thriving in social settings lies with you. When you accept this message, you empower yourself to make that transformation from a shy introvert into a confident one. But before you consider coming out of your shell and stepping into a world of adventures, it is important to understand where you are coming from. You must know exactly what you face and then create a plan that will help you achieve your social goals. Science has shown us that we are more in control of our behavior. When we realize and accept that this is a good thing, we unlock a door to a whole new universe. The next thing on our to-do list is to uncover those uncomfortable truths about shyness.

Types of Shyness

When I was doing my research on this topic, I found out that there are different types of shyness. I am only going to focus on just three because I feel that these are the more common ones and they were the types that were most relevant to me. Some people experience all three of these types of shyness listed here. While a lot of us suffer from the first one. The names of the type of shyness are self-explanatory but I am going to put a little bit of information about them so that you can truly understand where you fit in.

Permanent Shyness

This is the type of shyness where the sufferer also experiences intense anxiety whenever they are put in social situations. This crippling anxiety limits their ability to interact effectively with their peers and people in their circle. Permanent shyness is not linked to specific events or social situations. It happens whenever you participate or even entertain the thought of participating in a social setting. The problem with being diagnosed or identifying with something permanent is that it can make it seem as though change is not possible. But this is not the case here. Permanent is not referring to the duration. It is talking about the circumstances in which the shyness occurs. Permanent shyness or not, you can change the situation because shyness is mostly a trait that you learn as you grow. I will get into more details on this in subsequent chapters.

Situational Shyness

This type of shyness is triggered by certain traumatic experiences from the past. Whenever you are put in a situation that bears any likeness or similarity with the previous traumatic experience, you would find yourself drawing back into yourself and shutting out the world. What happened in this instance is that the trauma you have experienced conditioned your mind to perceive certain circumstances as a threat to you. This in turn caused you to use shyness as a weapon to protect yourself and combat that situation. When shyness becomes a biological response to a specific situation, it becomes a part of your default setting whenever you are in an environment like the one that caused your initial trauma.

Transitional Shyness

Change is a very scary and intimidating prospect even for those who claim to live for it. When a rooster is suddenly put in a strange environment, you would observe that it stands on one foot and stays that way until it is certain of its environment before it places the second foot on the ground. Even then, that one foot would be quick to go up whenever it senses something unfamiliar. Being put in a new situation can cause you to be shy. This type of shyness is called transitional shyness. Think of your first day in a new school and how difficult it was to make new friends and meet new people. Even your first day at work is bound to be a trigger for transitional shyness. A lot of people suffer from this.

Now that we know the three common types of shyness, let us try and find out if being shy has any perks.

The Ups and Downs of Being Shy

People tend to look at shyness as a restrictive factor and in some ways, it can hold you back but only if you let it. In this segment, I want to help you look inwards to find the beauty and strength in your shyness. You may have witnessed the downsides of being shy but trust me there are a lot of benefits. I am certain that you bought this book because of the struggles you are having with your shy condition. So you may be already intimately familiar with the trials of being shy. But let me assume that you bought this book for someone else who is going through the situation. You want to be able to understand them better. The downsides of being shy include the inability to advocate for yourself, the absence of relationships that could be beneficial to you, missed valuable opportunities that you could have used to expand your experience and grow, etc. In short, shyness can stop you from achieving your true potential in life.

But being a shy person is not all doom and gloom. Regardless of what type of shyness you have, if you learn to understand what it is, you can harness it and make it work for you. This may sound like some psychological babble but it is a fact. Like many weaknesses people have learned to empower through knowledge, you can also do the same for shyness. But in its raw state, here are some of the many benefits that being shy offers you;

1. The ability to form genuine connections with people

As a shy person, being around just about anyone is not your prerogative. You don't just talk to people for talking sake. There is always a purpose to your socializing. This means that when you finally meet someone with whom you share a bond, you are in a better position to connect with them for genuine reasons and not just for social climbing or other petty things that make people form meaningless friendships.

2. You are more thoughtful and considerate with your words

As a social outlier, you understand the power that words have. You have had days where a simple smile from a random stranger and genuine concern expressed by the people you meet uplift you. So you also know that using your words flippantly can cause harm to the next person. Being shy causes you to be naturally thoughtful and this trait is extended to the way you use your words with people.

3. You are familiar with your own company

Being familiar with your company and enjoying your company are two different things entirely. However, I brought this here because a lot of extroverts and social butterflies tend to hide from their own company. The constant drive to be in the presence of other people is sometimes powered by their fear of being alone. As a shy person, you have already faced down this fear. The next step is for you to learn to enjoy your company.

When You Suffer from Extreme Shyness

One of the types of shyness I didn't mention in the previous segment is extreme shyness or social anxiety disorder. It is also referred to as social phobia this form of shyness is rooted in the fear of socializing. While many people worry about being awkward in social settings, a person who suffers from SAD is usually so crippled by their fear that they are unable to leave their houses. Diagnosing social phobia is easy, however, the treatment is the part that becomes complicated. This is because there are sufferers of this social anxiety disorder who can be treated through cognitive behavioral therapy. In other words, they would have to unlearn some habits and behavioral patterns that they have picked up over the years.

For some others, it is just helping them cope with that social awkwardness by teaching them socializing skills that they desperately need. The moment they master this, the phobia will reduce drastically. And for others, they would require in addition to the things I have mentioned here medication to stabilize their moods and regulate the chemicals in their brain that trigger the fear emotion anytime they are in public. If your fear of embarrassment or public ridicule is forcing you to avoid doing things or even talking to people, you may have a social anxiety disorder. If social embarrassment also ranks high as one of your worst fears, you might have a social anxiety disorder. Being shy can leave you tongue-tied in situations where you are supposed to speak up for yourself. But having social phobia will cause you to physically run at the prospect of speaking to someone for any reason.

If you fall in this category, in addition to a lot of the things that I am going to list in this book, one of the things you would need to do is to speak to a psychologist or a psychotherapist. They would help to diagnose your condition and then determine what kind of treatment would help. You might require medication, therapy, or both. The important thing is at the end of the day, you are getting the help you need so that you can start living the life that you want. As you continue your search for the right therapist for you, you can continue reading the rest of this book because they are tips that can help you build your social skills which will help improve your social experiences generally. What you are going through as a SAD sufferer is very difficult but I believe that you can overcome this and become better for it.

Having proper knowledge of a problem is usually the first step in finding the solution for it. Hopefully, from the information in the chapter, you have a better understanding of what is going on inside of you. Most importantly, I hope that you were able to grasp the "seed" information which is that you are in control. Therefore, you can determine the social experiences that you have going forward. Of course, your ability to control your fear is not going to happen overnight. It is going to require deliberate and conscientious effort on your part. But speaking from experience, all that work is going to be worth it at the end of the day. Now that you know what you are dealing with, let us look at how it affects you.

Chapter Two

Coping with Shyness in Public

There are social expectations that everyone must strive to meet up to. The rebel in me sometimes wants to break the rules but if you want to make it far in life, you have to learn to get along with people. As much as we hate it, getting along with people does require playing by the rules. But what happens when those rules cause your lungs to constrict in fear and keeps you from playing the field? Shyness in public is often brought on by pressure to fulfill certain social roles. We fear that we would fumble, do or say the wrong thing that will cause people to ridicule, reject or refrain from ever dealing with us again. But are your fears real? Do they truly have that much power over you? Let us find out.

Social Phobia and Other Fears that Hold You Back

The fears that we have are sometimes genetically encoded. The fight or flight syndrome that we have comes from distant memories passed down to us by our ancestors. Social phobias on the other hand are an acquired experience. You either inherit those fears through a third party or a direct experience. Most times, our social fears come from a negative childhood experience that was so traumatic, it triggered our survival instincts. These fears can also be formed in your adult years. Whether it happened in your childhood or your adult years, there is a root memory. The negative experiences you have will only serve to affirm your fears and build on your social habits.

When you have a negative social experience that shocks you to the core, your brain registers this information by mapping out the factors that led to the threat in the first place. One key element that would be identified is the people involved in that initial incident. Your brain tells you that this person could potentially cause you harm. The more the focus on that memory, the more you feed the negative elements until it gets to a point where it is not just the people involved initially that become a threat. The message you get mentally is that people are a threat. When you internalize such a message, you start withdrawing from people. Small talk becomes tedious because all the while you are chatting with them, your brain is raising all sorts of alarms about the dangers that you face. This leads to an anxiety attack. The only reprieve would be retreating to your world away from people.

This is an extreme case. In mild cases, you consider yourself too insignificant or not worthy enough to offer any valuable contribution to the conversation. Again, you voluntarily put yourself on the sidelines and shut yourself inside your head. This habit of retreating into your shell whenever you are in the midst of people becomes so addictive that you can sometimes manifest physical symptoms of your shyness. Sweaty palms, nausea, decreased or increased breath sounds...do any of these sound familiar? To put everything I have said so far in perspective, your fears are borne from a negative memory (could be something you experienced directly, could be something that happened to someone that you know) and what you feel when you are in public is not an actual real-time experience. It is your brain replaying an incident and keeping you trapped in that memory.

Understanding Physical Symptoms of Shyness and Social Triggers

Shyness goes beyond feeling reluctant to speak to people. That blush spreading on your cheek or the hairs rising at the back of your neck when someone says hello to you is not an instant signal that your shyness is problematic. Those are natural reactions truth be told. What is not natural is throwing up right before you are called to speak on stage. In this segment, I will help you identify those symptoms and possibly the things that trigger them so that you are better able to manage them and be in better control. Let us start by analyzing the symptoms that you experience and what they could mean for you. Our aversion to speaking in public causes different types of reactions ranging from nausea to skin rash. I have heard of cases where some people pass out. The root cause of the symptoms you are experiencing is stark fear.

Fear is an emotion you experience when there is a presence of danger or threat to harm your person. For someone who is struggling with the fear of public speaking, what has happened is that your brain has turned public spaces where people are present into a battle zone. It looks for specific things that trigger your fears which will, in turn, activate those symptoms that you experience. Your typical reaction to fear is to run away from the danger which will further affirm your brain's perception of public speaking spaces as danger zones. All of this leaves you trapped in a recurrent cycle. The root cause of shyness and fear of public speaking are variations of this process I have just laid out for you. The key to breaking that cycle is identifying the elements that trigger your fears and then taking the steps to reframe those fears.

Let us assume that your fear is linked to an image of you embarrassing yourself most horrifyingly in front of everyone. Your key trigger would be the podium you are to climb on. Reframing that podium as a platform that provides a safe space for you to air out your opinions instead of seeing it as a disaster waiting to happen can help ease the tension and get you through your ordeal. I recently heard someone describe anxiety as being stuck in the future. This is true in this case. You are concentrating on the negative things that could potentially happen rather than looking at the opportunity presented to you right now. You have to stop reacting to the future if you want to overcome your social fears. Whether it is fear of how people would react to you or fear of poor performance, dwelling on the potential negative will only serve to slow down your ability to achieve your social goals.

Hanging Out With Strangers Vs a Familiar Crowd

When you watch me interacting with people I consider my close friends and then Juxtapoz that with my interaction among strangers, it is like watching two different people operate with the same face and body. Even I am baffled by this difference in my personality. Granted, we tend to be more civil with strangers than people we call family but in an introvert's case, this behavior is extreme. I am highlighting it here because I believe that you can be very sociable. There are some in the introverted community who have no friends whatsoever and have little to no interaction with family members. But even they have a "circle" whom they let their guard down a little bit for.

If you take the time to really observe your interactions with people in a familiar setting, you might be able to uncover one of the keys to unlocking your sociable side. The major difference between strangers and familiar people when you are talking about socializing is the fact that you have been able to establish a safe space with one group. Remember what we learned about fear in the last segment and how it triggers your reactions. If you can somehow learn to carry that safe space with you instead of associating it with faces, you would successfully solve at least 50% of the problem you are struggling with. There is safety in familiarity but it does not guarantee that those things you fear cannot happen in these familiar circles.

Stop looking at every interaction as a potential disaster. But most importantly, stop looking at every social disaster as the end of the world. I will go into details on this later in the book but I want you to know that rejection, opposition, or even a little slip in public does not define you for the rest of your life. Choosing to strictly interact with people in your circle is life choosing to live life in a bubble. It is restrictive and not realistic. Of course, it makes sense to stay closer to people who make you feel safe. But if the fear of some social harm is keeping you from expanding that circle and creating richer experiences, you are doing it wrong. That girl or boy you admire are strangers now but after a few social interactions, they could be the people who would positively change your life forever. And even if they turn out to be weirdos or turn you down initially, your potential to thrive and succeed is going to be impacted by this...not without your permission at least.

5 Rules for Managing Social Anxiety

Before we get into the rules for managing social anxiety, let us take a look at what you have learned so far to give you a little bit of perspective on the next task you would have to set for yourself.

1. Your fear is drawn from a previous memory and not an ongoing experience

2. Limiting your interactions to familiar people is only going to limit your life experiences

3. Fear is what triggers your reactions. Facedown your fears and the story will change.

Now that we have gotten that out of the way, let us look at the rules for managing your anxiety when you are in public.

1. Rule One: Do not dismiss your fear

Your fear is valid. Even though it is rooted in an experience, it is still as real as your hands in front of your face. To regular folks who don't have the same fears as you, what you feel might be called silly and unreasonable. Don't buy into that. Take it seriously.

2. Rule Two: Take baby steps

You might be feeling frustrated with your current dilemma and probably wish to turn things around as soon as possible. But taking leaps that you are not ready for will only throw you deeper into your social anxiety. Learn to be extremely patient with yourself.

3. Rule Three: Ask for help

Your struggles with social anxiety can make you feel isolated but some battles are not meant to be fought alone. Being strong and independent has nothing to do with suffering alone. When you feel overwhelmed, it is okay to admit that you are not okay.

4. Rule Four: You need to be your hero

Coming from a rule that says you should ask for help, this might seem to contradict. But here's the thing, if you are sitting around waiting for someone to recognize your pain and save you from it, you might have to grab a cushion and get comfortable in that chair. The only person that can change your situation is you.

5. Rule Five: Just do it

Walking up to a model at a party and telling her that I liked her was seizure inducing act at one point in my life. I had 10,000 reasons not to but I drew courage from the practice runs I had (we will talk about this) and I walked up to her even though even bone in my body turned to jelly at the thought. We ended up dating for a few months and remain very good friends to this day. Imagine what would have happened if I had chickened out.

Overcoming your social struggles will require a process. You are not going to suddenly wake up one day and be comfortable enough to talk in front of people without starting the process now. I find that coming to terms with who you are as an individual plays a crucial role and that is what we are going to focus on next.

Chapter Three

Becoming Your True Self

The biggest and most impactful figure in your journey to building a social network and improving your interactions with people is you. But sometimes, being "you" can be a tough job. Especially when you are not impressed with what you see in the mirror every day. I had a friend called Chad. We weren't exactly buddies but we ran in the same circles from kindergarten and he was one of the few people who went out their way to say hello and check on me. Chad was a smart, funny, and very sociable person. He dressed sharp and had the warmest laugh. He set up a bakery after college, married a few years later, and had a beautiful family. Even after I moved to another city, he tried to stay in touch. The incredible thing about Chad is that I wanted to be him so badly. And every social faux pas I committed was measured against the incredible personality of Chad. We all have a Chad in our lives. But as amazing as Chad is, being the real you is a hundred times better than being Chad. Read on to understand why.

Being Unapologetically You

There was a point on my journey to becoming more socially outgoing where I was depressed. I had done a complete closet overhaul and started dressing like models straight out of fashion magazines. My hair was coiffed to perfection. My teeth sparkled like polished marbles. My social etiquette could land a seat among the royals and I would fit in perfectly. I had nailed the smile, the expressions and had even recorded some social successes. But I was unhappy. Every time I had to put on my high fashion clothes and outside face, I experienced anxiety attacks. This bothered me because I finally looked like I fit in with the crowd that I was so desperate to impress. So, why was I still struggling?

My therapist said something profound that shook me (they tend to do that). She said it is because you are faking being yourself. At first, I thought, what?! How do I fake being myself? Then I realized that I had fooled myself into thinking that all these things I had learned, bought, and become were the things that I truly wanted. And I did this because I measured myself against the standard set by other people rather than the standards I had set for myself. I wanted to be like Chad when I should have worked on being like me. Being yourself focuses on extracting information about yourself and acting on that information. It meant looking inward and discovering the things that made me genuinely happy.

Getting to know yourself would mean spending time with yourself. You would think that as an introvert, I would have this part nailed down but the truth is that we often spend time with ourselves focusing on how other people are living. We think so much about what they want, what they like, and how they are generally that we fail to pay attention to what we like. What styles make you feel most confident? How do you genuinely like to spend your time if fear was not a factor in your day-to-day living? That answers that you get might surprise you and spur you into taking actions that align with your true nature. Before you step out into the world to build genuine connections with other people, you have to forge a genuine relationship with yourself.

Letting Go of Social Labels and Expectations

There are millions of words that can be used to describe who we are but we tend to spend time obsessing over specific labels and finding our identity in them. Generally speaking, this shouldn't be much of a problem except that, we are focusing on the labels thrust on us by society. Every decade or so, there are specific labels that become socially trendy and we all get swept up in the hype trying to fit into these labels. We want to be hippie, nerdy, alpha, bossy, modern and so much more. If the label that aptly describes you does not fit into any of the trendy ones, we start "fixing" ourselves. The objective is to gain the approval of the public which we feel (mistakenly so) is essential for building quality relationships.

Don't get me wrong. Acceptance is important for forging good relationships but the focus should be on people accepting you for who you are rather than who you project yourself to be. When you step up to a person wearing the wrong label, you come off as fake and people tend to sense the fakery and react to it. Even if you can successfully fool everyone, you cannot fool yourself. As you take the plunge to build your social credibility by getting to know who you are, try not to use social standards as your model. It is perfectly okay to draw inspiration from people and emulate certain amiable qualities but let that process not be about wanting to fit it. Let it be about doing something that genuinely makes you happy.

From childhood, certain labels would have been thrown at you and as you get older, you find that some of those labels stick. This is not because it aptly captures your personality. It is a projection of other people's perception of you. In some cases, this mislabelling stunts your social growth. To change that, you have to start unlearning some things and dropping those labels along the way. This may not be easy as you might have formed some emotional attachments to these labels. However, to instigate the kind of change you want to see in your personality and become the kind of person that people enjoy being around, you may have to make some painful changes. This is one of those cases where I would say change is definitely a good thing.

Risks You Must Learn to Take

When we are put in a social situation, one thing that could trigger our fear is rejection. You have made all this effort to become more socially acceptable only to have someone turn you down. It is devastating every time you experience it, especially if this was something you were particularly interested in getting a yes for. But this is a risk that must be taken when you socialize. Why do we put ourselves through rejection? Why not lock yourself in and stay indoors? Well, it is the same reason players get on the field, suffer defeat at the hands of their opponents and still step out to play the next game with excellence. It is all a part of the game.

Nobody is universally liked. Sure, some people might attract the like button more than others but you will always five a community who would give them a thumbs down without even blinking. The same thing can be said for socializing. Not everyone is going to appreciate you, accept you or even like you. And this is not something you can or should even try to control. Whether it is a business or romantic proposal, no matter how well prepared you are, you always run the risk of getting rejected. The problem is that we have a bad habit of taking rejection personally. Yes, rejection can leave you feeling dejected but it does not and should not define your next pitch. I am sure you have heard stories of how people like Walt Disney were turned down several times before they finally got the right yes that catapulted them into their desired destinies. You are not going to be the first person to get a no from people and it is highly unlikely that you would be the last.

The key to moving past a painful rejection is understanding that it is not about you but the other person. There are lessons you could pick from the experience that might help you in your next social encounter. In a business situation, perhaps your research did not fully cover the scope of the other party's expectations. That was a mistake that can be fixed and not a defining character flaw so once again, it is not about you. Keep your focus on the lesson you learned, pay attention to the things you got right, and then put yourself in the mindset to do it all over again but better the next time. You might get no a few more times but always remember that getting the affirmative (yes) will make everything worth it. My favorite quote of all time is this; you can't fail if you keep trying.

Reframing Your Past Experiences

The final bit in this process of becoming you is reframing your past experiences. We know that our fears are shaped by these experiences so if you can somehow put what you have been through in a new frame, you can get your social anxiety under control. Reframing your experiences does not mean you should erase what happened to you. That is unhealthy and could lead to a whole new set of mental and emotional issues. What I am talking about is limiting that singular experience to a moment in time rather than setting it up to be a continuous fixture whose impact extends into your future. Another element that needs to be reframed in that experience is your role in it.

Oftentimes, in our past negative experiences, we focus on the details that rendered us powerless and helpless. Rehashing these details will only affirm our helplessness causing you to feel like a victim all over again. What we do not take into account is the fact that surviving trauma requires strength. You may not like how you have survived but the fact is that you did. That alone elevates you above the helplessness that you felt. With the limited information that you have, you have managed to make a life for yourself and all the steps you have taken so far have brought you to this point of transformation. This makes you uniquely powerful and strong.

Strength is not only in your muscular structure or heroic deeds. It is in your ability to wake up and make something for yourself. The fact that you now dare to desire something better for yourself is a testament to your strength. Yes, you are scared. Yes, you have a dark past. But you are more than these feelings. You are more than your history. Put this memory and the emotions that it has stirred firmly in your past. Take whatever lessons you can from the experiences. Remind yourself that even though this experience was powerful, you have something even more powerful and that is choice. You have the choice to live above the fear and allow your true self to shine through and prevail.

After coming to terms with who you truly are, the next step is finding the confidence to put yourself out there in social settings. In the last three chapters including this one, our focus has been on changing the message from the inside. Now, we are going to put that message into action on the outside so that you become more effective in your communication, establish connections with people, and learn how to grow your relationships from there.

Chapter Four

Confidence Building Techniques

Confidence is a major missing ingredient when it comes to shy people talking to other people. One of the reasons our confidence takes a back seat is because we mentally dumb down our ability to communicate effectively. When you talk down on yourself whether you are feeding off information that was given to you a long time ago or some negative experience in the past, you are sanding away your confidence and if you continue doing this for a long time, you end up with very poor self-esteem. This restricts your ability to walk up to anyone to strike a conversation. But today, all of that is going to change. At the end of this chapter, you are going to learn how to tune out the confidence zapping voices and focus on empowering yourself mentally and emotionally.

5 Ways to Fake Your Confidence

There are a couple of things that are okay to fake and your confidence is one of them. You are not going to wake up one morning suddenly feeling extremely confident enough to socialize the way you want. This is something that you have to build over time. In the initial stages, when you are taking those tiny baby steps, you would need tons of confidence to pull through and confidence is not always easy to acquire. However, you can psych yourself into believing that you are confident and with time, you will become confident.

Up next are five ways to fake your confidence but I want you to know that even as you are carrying out these five things, your hands might still feel shaky, your heart rate will still be very fast and sometimes you may even feel like you're about to die of thirst. You have to ensure that these physical symptoms do not stop you from pursuing your social goals. Just show up and push through. When you do it once, you have the courage to do it again until it becomes natural to you.

1. Dress to look the part

When you wear an outfit that you like it feeds your confidence. However, you have to try and ensure that you are balancing what you like with the image you want to put out to the world. If you are like me, you would know that nothing screams comfort like a pair of yoga pants. But when you are in a business meeting, you have to go for something a little bit more upscale. Choose an outfit that portrays your style accurately. It would inject some faux confidence into your attitude.

2. Strike a pose

Nothing screams poor confidence like a person who is slouching and dragging themselves with a droopy head. Maintaining a straight posture with your chin up can make a huge difference in how you perceive yourself. Whether you are going in for a business meeting or are out on a date with a potential romantic prospect, keeping a confident pose can help you fake your confidence even though you don't feel it.

3. Practice good hygiene and grooming

they say that looking good is good business but looking good goes beyond wearing the most expensive or trendy outfit it is something as basic as taking a nice clean bath wearing deodorant doing a thorough routine every morning and ensuring that your hair and nails are kept in good condition these little details help you feel more confident about yourself.

4. Focus on what you have

Poor self-esteem happens for a lot of reasons. One of them is focusing on your deficits or weaknesses. We tend to ignore the amazing talents and gifts that we have and obsess over what we think we should have but don't. If you are going to fake your confidence successfully, you must start looking at what is working for you and keep your focus on that.

5. Practice your confidence speech

What does confidence look like to you? Now imagine yourself wearing this confidence comfortably and try to emulate it in front of a mirror. If you have dinner plans or a business meeting coming up, practicing a few lines in front of the mirror can help you become familiar with the role of confidence that you are trying to project. Thus, helping you to fake it even though you don't feel it yet.

Healing From Past Social Trauma

When you find yourself dealing with social anxiety that has roots in a traumatic experience you are facing a two-pronged problem. This is because on one hand, you have the trauma that needs to be resolved and on the other hand, you have the social anxiety that came out of that trauma. Our reaction to either of these situations can vary in degree and depths. As a shy person, it is typical that your reaction was to withdraw yourself as a defensive mechanism to protect you from any future recurrence. The problem with this sort of reaction is that you are hiding yourself away from the future while constantly living in the past.

If any of these describes you, it is time for you to shake that off and put yourself out there. We talked about this in the previous chapter. There is always going to be a risk. The life that we live in the world today is not perfect. It is full of ups and downs. You can do your best to ensure that you do not knowingly put yourself in situations that will result in physical or emotional harm. But outside of this, you must learn to accept that this experience is over and done with and that the only reason it has power over you right now is that you continue to allow it. When you were going through this traumatic experience, the ranges of emotions that you felt were intense and this perhaps led you to the wrong conclusion that you have lost absolute control over everything. But this is a lie you must stop telling yourself if you want to heal and resolve this issue.

Somehow, you may have convinced yourself that your struggles with social anxiety or shyness are not directly linked to a trauma you may have experienced growing up. Still, the truth is that our past affects us in more ways than we realize and so to heal from it, the first place to start is acceptance. You must accept that you have something you are struggling with and then the next place is to either talk to a professional about it or see if you can talk to someone in your circle of trust who has your best interest at heart. Talking about it can help expose those areas where you have been most impacted by the trauma. It can also help you make sense of what has happened and see a clear path as to how to move on going forward. I also want you to understand that having a traumatic past does not necessarily mean you are damaged. People avoid the trauma of their past because they want to avoid this label. It is possible that your upbringing may have caused a trauma that triggered your social anxiety. There is no shame in this. Accept this and you can kick-start the process of healing.

Stepping Out of Your Comfort Zone

Shyness is about operating from a place of safety. Strangers and people with who you do not have a direct day-to-day relationship with represent danger for you. So subconsciously, you choose to stay in this space that makes you feel safe and comfortable. The problem with living in your comfort zone is that it can hold you back from making progress. If you are going to take off the garment of social reclusiveness and dip your toes into relationships with people whether for business or romantic purposes, you need to step out of your comfort zone. But in doing this, you must know that stepping out of your comfort zone does not mean you are stepping into the fire. I believe that it is a mindset like this that keeps you trapped within this safe space you have created for yourself.

Your comfort zone is not really about protecting yourself. It is about fear. You have created this narrative that everything outside the safe space is going to endanger you. This feeds your fear and drives your father and father into your comfort zone. To halt this process and become a person who is okay with taking risks, you have to first come to terms with the truth about yourself. You are afraid and it is okay. Walking up to a total stranger who you feel intimidated by is scary for anyone even for the most confident people. However, the difference between confident people and yourself is the fact that they take that step. No one knows what the outcome is going to be when you attempt to socialize. You can only trust that you put yourself out there and open yourself to the possibility of gaining the rewards of this action. Being afraid does not make you less of a person. But by allowing your fear to control you can guarantee that the rich and positive experiences you have in life are far lesser than you deserve.

After confronting the truth about your feelings, your next move is to put yourself in a mental state of mind to take that first step. When it comes to socializing, taking the first step is probably going to be one of the most difficult decisions and by taking this first step, I am referring to putting yourself in an actual situation where you are forced to socialize or talk to someone. Just make sure that you are taking baby steps. For someone who has a fear of height, jumping out of a plane in a parachute without any preparation is only going to amplify that fear or bring it to life. This is because they are not mentally or emotionally ready for it. Start with little things like smiling at strangers, exchanging contacts at business meetings, or even striking a 30-second to a 1-minute conversation with someone randomly. Those first few steps are going to be awkward and you might feel as though your heart is jumping out of your mouth. But when you have successfully done this two or three times, you will receive a confidence boost that would reflect in your socializing skills. So you see, stepping out of your comfort zone has a lot of benefits. Focus on these benefits as your third steps in this journey and you are well on your way to becoming a social risk-taker.

The Power of Affirmations

The food that you consume consistently will determine your physical health. The words that you ruminate on consistently will determine your mental health. Positive affirmation is a topic that gets me excited because I have experienced the power of positive thinking and positive speaking. My entire success is rooted in my ability to define my world through my words. This might seem like an impossible feat but it's just the truth. When you are talking about reframing past experiences, channeling your emotions, and unlearning bad social behavior, speaking powerful words that resonate with your being can be a powerful motivator.

Positive affirmations are designed to confirm, affirm and define your expectations for the future. It is a way that you can consciously and deliberately train yourself to focus on the positives in life. Sometimes, our ability to socialize effectively is rendered useless by the negative thoughts and words that we use to describe ourselves. Here you may have told yourself that you are not good enough or that you are not capable of accomplishing the things that you want to accomplish. Unfortunately, it doesn't just stop there. You go on to act on these negative words you have spoken. For example, because you have told yourself that you are not good enough, you avoid talking to people in general even when you have some genuine fondness for a few people. Positive affirmations as a way to reverse this negative habit.

With positive affirmations, you empower yourself to take action on the good thoughts that you have developed about yourself. So when you have a positive affirmation that says I am strong or I am good enough, you are forced to consciously and subconsciously act on these words that you have spoken. This is why it is important to make positive affirmations a part of your routine. If you are going to build your confidence, you need to affirm your strengths and your expectations so that they can become your reality. To create your positive affirmations you must know that grammar is not a prerequisite. It is more important to prioritize your connection to the words that you are speaking over the sentence structure. If you are feeling uninspired, you can look to the negative words you have spoken about yourself for inspiration. So if you are fond of telling yourself things like, I am not good enough to talk to this person, your positive affirmation could be I am more than enough. Take those seeds of doubt, fear, and emotional insecurity into account. You can write it down so you can see what you have been saying about yourself. Next, put a positive spin on those words and then use them to affirm what you expect for the future whenever you want or feel down.

These steps that I have listed in this chapter will not turn you into a social butterfly overnight. But if you are consistent and committed to the practice, it soon becomes a habit and when it becomes a habit it becomes a way of life for you. The bottom line is, you can be so much more than you have ever imagined. All you have to do is find the courage to connect with the person that lies buried inside of you. Awaken that powerful being through words and actions that align with what you hope to have.

Chapter Five

Striking Conversations in Romantic Situations

When you are shy, being in the presence of someone with who you would like to get intimate can compound the situation especially, in the early stages. In this chapter, we are going to look at how you can hold a conversation under romantic circumstances like a date. You are also going to get tips and ideas on romantic conversation starters that you can use to either ask a person out or simply keep the conversation going to the point where they become interested in you.

Be the Person You Want to Date

One mistake that introverted people make when it comes to their romantic lives is keeping the focus on the other person. They put their romantic interest on an unrealistic pedestal and use this as a yardstick to measure their worth. This unnecessary comparison puts a lot of pressure that makes you second guess yourself at every turn. Even when they are in a relationship, they still consider themselves unworthy. A mindset like this is a great breeding ground for poor self-esteem and low confidence issues which can lead to toxic insecurities. No relationship can survive toxic insecurities and when they come to an end, the cycle repeats itself in a new relationship.

To improve the quality of your relationship or give your personality a romantic boost, you need to turn the gaze on you. Ask yourself the question, what are you bringing to the table? The reason for this is that by turning the focus on yourself, you allow yourself to build on qualities and character traits that make you more likable and approachable. In trying to answer this question, you must ensure that you are not focusing on just your weaknesses. Look at those qualities that people genuinely admire in you. If you have the opportunity to build yourself from the scratch, what are those things you would like to change about yourself? When you get the answers, also ask yourself, can those things be changed? If they cannot, you must learn to accept yourself for who you are. As for the things that can be changed, for example, your weight or personal style, you can go ahead and create a low-pressure plan to initiate that change. One thing you must do in this process is to ensure that the standards you are creating are not measured by what society considers good or sexy. Let it be something that you are comfortable with.

The closer you are a physical representation of the type of person you would like to be, the more confident you will feel. When you are confident, you are more articulate and eloquent in romantic situations. Of course, there are still a lot of other things that you need to work on but getting this out of the way would make that process easier for you and also more natural. I am not saying that your life has to be perfect and in order before you consider dating someone. However, when you are in a place where you are comfortable with who you are as a person and you love yourself, you create the right environment for a relationship to thrive. Let us not forget that the other person had to do their work as well. But you doing your part means that the job is already halfway done.

10 Things Not to Say to "the One"

When you meet someone you like and for some crazy reason they've accepted to go out with you, it is easy to become a little drunk with words. You start picturing this amazing future with them and this can cause you to get carried away. Many people have suffered a nasty case of verbal diarrhea as a result of this. The nervousness and anxiety from being in the presence of this person in combination with excitement about your future can cause you to say more than what you intended. Oftentimes, those things that are said are not good. In romantic settings, a little bit of awkwardness is allowed sometimes it's even considered cute but going overboard with your declarations of love might end up with your date dumping you. Avoid that situation with my foolproof 10-point list of what not to say.

1. **You are not the type of person I would normally date**

   This implies that they might not be your first option which is very discouraging. Instead, you could try saying something like; all of this is a bit new for me.

2. **You look too cute to be single**

   his is a backhanded compliment. It may sound as though you are offering them a compliment but it also implies that something might be wrong with them. A better way to say this would be; you are beautiful.

3. **I think I love you**

   I do not doubt that you may have said these words from a sincere and genuine place in your heart. But saying this out loud on a date with someone you don't know very well may seem as though you use the word, "love" flippantly. Until you are in a more secure place with this person, I would say keep this information to yourself.

4. **My ex was a.../my ex used to say...**

   You are on the cusp of starting something new. Dragging past experiences into a date can make it seem as though you are still attached to that past. Refrain from making any references to a previous relationship. Make it all about your partner in the present.

5. **My therapist says...**

Whatever happens between you and your therapist should remain between the both of you. Even in relationships that you have established trust in, referring to conversations that you have with your therapist in this way can make you seem incompetent. Let your opinions and perspectives come from you instead of a third party.

6. **How many dates have you gone on lately?**

This is a question that I'm sure you are dying to find the answers to. However, you should refrain from asking these types of questions as it forces your date to bring in their past experience into your present situation. Also, if you are being honest with yourself, the answer might be scary.

7. **I think Jeffery Epstein is misunderstood**

You may have strong political and social opinions on issues that are very relevant to everyone. And those opinions may be valid to you but your romantic interest may not be the best person to have that conversation with. Especially when you are on a date. Focus on getting to know them.

8. **Maybe, I am kinda, sorta into that...**

Using terms like "maybe, kinda, sorta" in your conversation with your date will make you seem unsure and inconsistent. All of that just screams low confidence. You try saying something like, "I am not sure" instead.

9. **I am a broke, loser living with my parents**

As I said earlier, awkward social situations can lead to verbal diarrhea like this one. Apart from the fact that throws you in a completely negative light words like there's have negative energy that can bring down the tone of the entire evening. Maintain an optimistic attitude.

10. **So, where do you see this relationship going in 5 years?**

If you were asking this type of question in a job interview situation, it would be appropriate. But on a date, this is too much pressure. Avoid anything marriage-related. Don't talk about kids, family members who they don't know about, and so on.

These rules written here are a list of things you should not do. This then begs the question, what can you do? Be yourself...the best version of yourself. Be kind. Be patient. Be a good listener. Offer meaningful compliments. Be sincere. Be courteous. And be calm. The goal is not to win the other person over. That is what you hope for but it should not be your goal. Instead, make it your mission to enjoy the evening. Focusing on the moment rather than winning the person can take the pressure off you and give the both of you a chance to truly connect.

The Art of Perfect Timing

When you watch actors on stage and how they interact with the audience, you would observe that the magic is not just in what they say and how they say it. It is evident in "when" they say it. Timing is very important when it comes to interacting with people. You have to know when to pause when to inject some humor and also want to simply sit back and listen to what the other person is saying. When your timing is off, you can end up with awkward silences which ruin the mood for a conversation or a situation where what you are trying to say gets lost in translation because you rushed your words.

Timing is not only linked to your speech. It has also been associated with nonverbal cues which play an important role in communication. Body language experts for example will tell you that holding eye contact for longer than 10 seconds with someone that you are just meeting for the first time is rude. A more appropriate way will be to give them a glance lasting for 2 or 3 seconds and then looking away. These simple details can enrich your communication and build a connection with the person you are trying to get romantically linked to. In subsequent chapters, I will go into more details about these body language cues and nonverbal communication tips. But for now, you must understand how to time yourself perfectly.

Unfortunately, the skill of timing is something that can only be acquired through practice. No amount of rehearsals in front of a mirror can adequately prepare you for timing. This is because you can't predict what the other person is going to say or how you're going to react to what you say. Another thing to note is that timing is numerical as well as it is visual. So the space that you are in could determine the tone of your conversation but even the topic of your conversation. Choosing the right place to meet up with your potential date can set the mood for the evening. Also picking the appropriate time for the date can make a difference. If you are going on a lunch date, go somewhere where the mood is light and cheery. If the person you're going to meet suggested somewhere fun and you are taking them to a place that is deep into the romance culture, you might be in for an awkward date.

You also need to read their mood and expressions if the person appears to be distracted and not in the right frame of mind for the date there is no shame in ending the outing before the predetermined time frame and perhaps suggesting another date. You could also offer an opportunity to cheer them up if they want. Don't make it your responsibility to change their mood. Offer to help. If they accept, use the time to do something creative. Remember, it is not about winning them over to your side. It's about enjoying the time that you have with them.

Social Cues You Should Pay Attention to

As introverts, we are often obsessed with all the reasons people may not like us that we fail to acknowledge the simple fact that we are very likable people. When you are put in a romantic situation, a lot of times you are given nonverbal pointers that indicate this person honestly likes you. Apart from this, you have to understand that our conversation requires a good listener, and part of being a good listener is paying attention to what the person is saying with the body language. But because you spend so much time in your head, you fail to see the signs. In this segment, I am going to point out some of those signs that indicate the true feelings of the person you are interacting with. My focus would be on signs that this person genuinely likes you. What you do with that information is entirely up to you. But having that information can be a major ego boost which is great for your confidence.

1. **They smile genuinely**

I am not talking about that tight-lipped type of smile. I am referring to the smile that stretches ear to ear and shows their front teeth. This smile says they are really into you or at least what you are saying.

2. **Their hands are visible**

   When people are not comfortable around you, they tend to close their fists. If they are not into you, they might cross their arms. This is a nonverbal way to say, stay away. When a person assumes this stance, do not try to touch them or enter their physical space.

3. **They lean forward to talk and listen to you**

   In a crowded place, this does not hold much weight. But if you are in a quiet and private place and they lean in or lean forward, it means that they are very interested in what you have to say.

4. **They cross their legs**

   This could go either way. This depends on what direction their upper body faces. If their legs are crossed and their upper body is facing away from you, they might be disinterested. If they are facing you, you might have a chance.

5. **Raised eyebrows with rapid blinking**

   Are you having an online date? Don't worry. The nonverbal cues on a person's face can tell you where their head is. If their eyebrows are slightly raised and they blink faster than normal, they might be feeling excited in a good way.

Now that you know a few subtle nonverbal cues, perhaps you can put them into practice. If you are in the habit of doing the opposite even when you like a person, this is a call to switch things up. If you are wondering what to do when a person's body shows that they are interested in you, just mirror them without being too obvious.

Chapter Six

How To Make Anyone Instantly Like You

If there is one superhuman power I wish I had, it would be the ability to make anyone I come across will like me. But since we do not live in the superhero universe, we have to find ways to become our superheroes. The title I used for this chapter is a bit misleading as it is impossible for everyone to like you and that should not be your objective. The goal is to figure out a way to get along with everyone. Some people are going to be more difficult than others to work with but you can still tolerate people's excesses and work with each other's strength to achieve a collective goal.

Become a Better Listener

Listening is a skill that every introvert has. This is because a lot of us naturally are not comfortable doing the talking. So we opt for our default mode which is to listen. But there is something about the way you listen that makes it difficult to carry on a conversation. It is possible to be present in a conversation and appear to be listening but your countenance and expression can make the talker feel as though you are trying to escape that conversation rather than paying attention to what they're saying. To foster a healthy relationship even though you are not contributing directly, you must know how to listen conversationally and that is what this segment is about.

1. **Tilt your head a little**

   Tilting your head a little to the left or the right is a universal body language that tells the person you are talking to, "Hey, I'm listening". It says you are engaged in that conversation and want to know more about what they are saying. It doesn't matter if the conversation is polite office gossip or a serious talk about the political climate in the country trying this simple move will make the person talking to you feel as though they are connected to you. The tilt should be slight and not too obvious.

2. **Avoid unnecessary eye movement**

   When someone is talking to you and your eyes are darting from place to place, what you're telling them indirectly with your current but the language is that you want to escape. The person talking to you will feel as though you would rather be anywhere else except where you are right now. Even if this is your true feeling, for the sake of getting along with people, it is important to act as though you are interested. This makes them feel valid and heard. Maintain eye contact when the person is talking and if you must remove your gaze, it should not linger too long on whatever it is you're staring at. Ensure that your focus is on them. If maintaining eye contact for too long makes you uncomfortable, you can choose to focus on something other than this person. The rest of your body language should tell them that you are engaged in the conversation.

3. **Animate your eye movement**

When you observe people interacting with each other the person who seems to be most engaged in a conversation is the one whose facial features are animated. When someone says something surprising, they mirror that in their expression and even though they don't say anything back. This expression alone validates what the other person has just said. To be a good listener, you have to emulate this type of behavior. Staring intently at the person talking to you is going to get awkward quickly. Instead, let the content of the conversation guide you on how to express what you are feeling. If the conversation is dull and boring, you can choose to alternate between squinting a little bit or relaxing your eyes, and occasionally raising your eyebrows. This transition in a movement will make the person you are listening to feel as though you genuinely care about what they say.

4. **Do not fold your arms**

When you feel defensive, crossing your arms is an instinctive reaction and the person you are talking to immediately sees this. Beyond the defensive stance, it also tells them that you are not open to what they are saying and makes you appear to be criticizing them even though you have not said a single word. A better approach would be to find a way to separate both arms. You could have one hand in my pocket and the other hand thoughtfully massaging your chin. This is a more engaging stance. Whatever you choose to do, try as much as possible not to fiddle with your hair tie or clothing. It can be interpreted as either being flirty, scared, or nervous. I am pretty sure that this is not the message you want to pass across especially when someone is confiding in you.

5. **Chip in occasionally**

A conversation is not meant to be one-sided and I understand talking as a shy person can require a lot of effort but when someone is talking to you as a good listener you have to respond verbally thankfully it doesn't have to be long sentences. Sometimes, saying "hmmm or mmhmm" at the right times can be sufficient. Expressions like, "Wow, I had no idea" or "That is interesting" can also be enough to convey your interest and attention to what they have said. One thing you should avoid doing unless they expressly ask for it is offering a solution in a way of telling them how you think they should handle their business. Even extroverts tend to make this mistake. Sometimes, people come to you just because they want to be heard not because they haven't figured out how to solve their problems. You coming up with a whole routine on how they should manage their situation can make it seem as though you are judgemental of their current choices. If they didn't ask for your advice, don't give it. And even if they do, be modest when you offer it.

Overcome the Hidden Language Barrier

All around us, hidden messages are being passed across and if you are blind to this language, you will miss out on a lot. Body language is another way we communicate and I am not just talking about how the other person responds to you. You have to understand that communication is a two-way street. There are certain things you are doing with your body language that might be sending out the wrong message to people. Your intention might be to open yourself more to connecting with people but your language could be saying stay away from me. This contradiction makes your journey to becoming more open and interactive with people difficult. People think the body language thing is a myth. But this is something that is used extensively by intelligence agencies like the CIA and the FBI.

During interrogation, the focus is not just on what the person is saying. They listen to and watch how this person says it with their body movements. This can help them detect where the person might be lying or it can also point out how big the issue is. We are not the FBI but we could learn a thing or two from some of their practices that can become very helpful in our day-to-day interaction. Understanding body language not only helps you understand the person better, but it can also alert you to potential danger and help you stay away from people who might be harmful. For example, people who have intense unanimated gazes tend to have a fetish for the darker things in life. People whose expressions only seem to light up when you experience some kind of physical pain might be into that S&M type of life. If neither of these things is important to you, I would say avoid such people.

In a previous segment, we covered a little bit about body language. I would advise that you do a little more research on the subject so that you can understand those signals that you might be given off that send a wrong message about you. But here are a few to get you started;

1. Try not to fidget when you talk to people. It would make it seem as though you have something to hide or that you lack confidence or that you are very nervous.

2. Do not enter people's personal space without their permission. In this instance, I am not referring to their bedroom or office. If a person is deliberately maintaining some distance between you and them, keep it that way.

3. Don't try to force a conversation when you see a person staring at the time or are busy looking at everyone else except you. You want to build a connection with people but ensure that you do it with people who are also interested in building that same connection with you.

Understand the Rules of Engagement

The fabric of our society is built on laws, rules, and regulations. As much as we are constantly encouraged to be ourselves, we have to confine this process within the laws of the land. I know that sounds drab and boring but it increases your chances of likability. Beyond that, it also makes you a person who is easy to work with. The importance of following the rules of engagement can make a difference in how many invites you get to events and activities with other people. You cannot expect to be invited to Buckingham Palace if you do not have simple table manners. I know you may not be aspiring to get there but you have to understand our journey in life is not hundred percent dictated by us. Sometimes, we are thrust into situations outside of our control and the only thing that we can regulate in such situations is our reaction to it. Whether you are in a romantic situation, social event or a business convention, these rules of engagement can help you get along swimmingly with everyone else.

1. **Dress the part**

   Showing up at a beach event in a three-piece suit will not score you any social points. You have to learn to dress appropriately for whatever occasion you are invited to. This doesn't always mean you have to be a part of the crowd. There are still ways to express your style while adhering to the rules that are in place. In fact, this is what is expected of you. Whenever you are going somewhere, always try to find out what the atmosphere is going to look like. This will determine how you should dress. Nine times out of ten, if you get your outfit right, everything else will fall in place.

2. Mind your language

Using swear words or talking to people in loud tones can be very off-putting. Even if this is you on a regular day, learn to curb this when you are out with people. The person sitting at the table next to you shouldn't hear what you are saying speak loud enough so that the people you are having a conversation with can hear you. Using curse words might be acceptable in your small circle but when you are out with other people you have to put a stopper on it.

3. Carry yourself with dignity

Slouching is a poor stance. Not only does it ruin your social chances, but it also causes body pain in the long run. Learn to stand tall and stand proud. This doesn't mean you should be stiff. You have to learn to balance being firm and fluid at the same time. The firmness in your stance says that you are confident. The fluidity of your body movement says that you are adaptable. Confidence and adaptability are excellent tools in any social setting.

Learn to Laugh at Yourself

Some of our social anxiety issues are born out of the fact that we take ourselves too seriously. We think that the world is waiting with bated breath over every step that we take. So if we stumble, we think the whole world is laughing but the stark reality is that people don't care. In a way, this knowledge can make you sad but that's a topic for another day. For now, allow this information to liberate you from the pressure you put on yourself to perform socially. There are simple rules that we have to learn to follow. We talked about them in the previous chapter. Stick to the rules and everything else comes easier to you. Even when you make a social faux pas like showing up at an event that specifically said "wear black and white" in a red dress, it doesn't mean that the world is at an end.

Mistakes or not social death sentences. They are simply lessons that you can use to help make yourself better. When they happen, don't take yourself too seriously. If people are pointing and laughing, sometimes it is okay to join in on the fun. People laughing at something that you did does not always mean there is malicious intent behind it. It could also be you did something ridiculous or funny. Laugh along. Being overly sensitive to things about yourself can make you a social pariah. This does not mean that it is okay for people to be cruel and malicious to you in the name of humor. You would have to learn to set boundaries for that. When you are on stage and you find yourself sweating and experiencing all the symptoms of anxiety, you could jokingly talk about it. I usually like to use phrases like, "Wow, who knew standing in front of a crowd could be so difficult". This doesn't send people into a laughing fit but it does cause some to smile and send the occasional understanding nods my way.

When you take yourself too seriously, you set up a standard for perfection and no one can ever meet up with the social standard for being perfect no matter how hard you try. Allow yourself to be who you are. As you make progress on your journey to becoming more open and trusting with people, accept that you are going to make some mistakes along the way and embrace them. You will not turn from the ugly duckling to a beautiful swan overnight. It is going to be a step-by-step journey. Embrace that process fiercely. When you are approaching someone to strike up a conversation with them and you find that the saliva in your mouth is tasting like metal, don't immediately give in to your instinct to power and slither away. Soldier on and see it through. You might offer a sweaty handshake and starter the first few sentences but you are making progress and that is what matters.

On a final note, it is important to have it on the back of your mind that people are not looking for a perfect human. They are looking for people they can relate to and believe it or not, a lot of people can relate with you when you are more authentic. Some people would try to bring you down but usually, that is just them projecting their insecurities on you. People will generally like you for who you are.

Chapter Seven

Reinventing Yourself Socially

I love the idea of reinventing yourself socially. Essentially, what you do is tear down those negative ideologies that you have about yourself and then put yourself together in the way that you want to be perceived by the rest of the world. It is an opportunity to affirm your strengths, work on your weaknesses and help you put your best foot forward every time. But before we get into the nitty-gritty details of this topic, I want you to remember this; the idea is not perfection. It is about perception.

Lead with Passion

When you are given an opportunity to start life over on a clean slate, it makes sense that you lean towards things that you are genuinely interested in. As opposed to working on things that you think people think you should be interested in. Do you see how weird that sounds? It is even weirder when you put it into practice. Allow your passion to be the driving force in your journey to reinventing yourself socially. If you are interested in art, pursue art-related events or programs. You are more likely to find people who share similar interests with you in such communities or gatherings. If business or music is your jam, look for circles that have those things as the theme. As a shy person who is choosing to step out of their shell, you have the rare opportunity to make deliberate choices about who and what you identify yourself with.

You should also try as much as possible not to concern yourself with what people are going to think of you. We live in an era where almost everything has a label attached to it and depending on who you are talking to, that label could be offensive or insulting. The fact is that you have to start learning to do you. People are going to talk anyway. So, wouldn't it be better to find yourself in a situation that you are completely happy with even though people are not? It is, for this reason, we started the book by looking inward. Start identifying with the things that bring you happiness and joy. Embrace things that bring up positive energy into your space and then move on to things that make every effort or action that you take worth it. As long as you are not hurting anyone else physically or emotionally, do you.

And speaking of hurting people emotionally, you have to understand that certain circumstances will require you prioritizing your own needs and wants above everyone else's. This does not make you selfish. If people are going to react negatively to you simply because you are indulging in something that empowers you positively, that is their problem. Don't feel pressured to do anything that you are not comfortable doing. Let your passion, interests, and motivation be your guide. It is interesting to note that when you are in a field or a space that is filled with things and you like and have a complete interest in, you are going to feel more confident about yourself and your surroundings. Having this feeling helps you to lose that self-consciousness that sometimes makes you socially awkward. This is a win-win situation if you ask me.

Strengthening Your Weaknesses

You are not going to be good at everything this is a simple fact of life and no matter how good you are there's always going to be some other person who is better at it than you this is another simple fact of life the sooner you accept this information the faster you can cut out those unnecessary struggles and focus on what is important in your bid to reinvent yourself. There might be areas where you feel you are not adequately equipped to cope. This is perfectly okay. It doesn't make you lesser than the next person. And if you are determined that this new image is what you want to present to the rest of the world, you must work on those areas you consider your weaknesses.

Perhaps you are not very articulate. You can start working on improving that area. If the problem has to do with your diction, watching English movies, reading books and articles online can help expand your vocabulary and this, in turn, will positively impact your diction. If you are struggling with conditions like stuttering or lisps, working with a speech therapist can help improve that situation. Nothing is unfixable if you put your mind to it. The objective of all of this is to get you closer to becoming the person you want to project to the world. If you feel that you are not a very fashionable person (I, myself struggled with this issue) reading fashion magazines, consulting with stylists, and so on can help you discover your style. Through the advice that they offer, you can build a wardrobe that best represents you while still helping you put   your   best   foot   forward.

Your weaknesses can be limiting but the boundary of those limitations is entirely dependent on you. I know of an incredible story of a mountain climber who got paralyzed during an expedition as a result of an accident. It took years for her to recover and even then she was bound to a wheelchair but that did not stop her from going on expeditions. She was able to accomplish more as a climber after her accident than she did before. The moral of that story is this; your weaknesses are only as limiting as you permit them to be. The internet is a huge source of information. Take advantage of this to find out how to manage whatever problems you think you have and create an action plan that will help you strengthen those areas. If it is a situation where you can work with a professional, I suggest that you do because they can provide a professional assessment of your performance. Sometimes those things you consider weaknesses might not be as bad as you think they are. Getting an expert opinion can help provide insights that would help develop an effective action plan.

The Illusion of Perfection

I have said this before and I will say it again. There is no such thing as perfection. Nobody is perfect. The only thing is perception. This person who you consider perfect has projected a persona that you now perceive as perfect. The reason it is impossible to attain perfection is simply because of our differences. No two humans are alike and therefore, our standards for measuring what success, excellence or greatness is will differ from person to person. The same goes for perfection. What might be perfect for you might be considered flawed by another person. It is for this reason you shouldn't concern yourself with other people's opinions about you. The only thing you should focus on is projecting an image of the person you want the world to perceive. What they do with the information is not your problem.

Pursuing perfection is unrealistic and unattainable. It puts excessive pressure on you which can lead to even more social performance issues. If you are called on to speak on stage, do not expect to sound like your favorite speaker. You may emulate his or her style in your speaking methods and this is okay. But wanting to become like them is unrealistic. I feel that every time I created an objective that was based on satisfying trivial and unnecessary things like garnering the approval of people, I lose track of the important stuff and fail miserably. However, if I focus on what I think is important like ensuring that the message is passed across if I am in a public setting or that I can put my name out there if I am at a networking event, I find that I can hit my goals effortlessly.

When reinventing yourself, keep your focus on what is truly important. Aim to add value not just to yourself but to the people that you meet. When you are setting expectations, make sure that they are realistic. Aiming to add value to every single person that you meet is a bit unrealistic and leans towards those perfectionist ideologies. Instead, your goal should be to be able to at least positively impact one person. When you train your focus on just this one person, the ripple effect of your efforts will expand to reach more people. When I am on stage, I don't try to talk to everyone at once. I feel like pieces of myself become scattered when I do that and this makes me disoriented. Instead, I try to imagine the audience as just this one person I am having a conversation with, and with this image in my mind, I can interact better with my audience. As we progress in the book, I am going to talk about public speaking. But for now, just know that focusing on what is important will help you reach your social goals faster.

Use Positive Reinforcements

Earlier on, I described how our brain draws on past experiences to formulate opinions about present circumstances which activate fear and cause you to flee social situations. With this information, I can assure you that you can also train your brain to associate social activities with positive emotions. When you have a positive social experience, try as much as possible to hold on to that. You can do this by reinforcing the feelings you are experiencing when you are in that moment. For example, when you take the first step to interact with a stranger and it is a positive experience, focus on how you feel in that moment and then smile. Allow the smile to linger for more than a moment. This simple act has informed your brain that a positive social experience just happened. The next time you come across a stranger you would draw on this positive memory to feed your present moment.

What this implies is that you have to take that first step. But remember, we are not doing the big things all at once. You can walk into your favorite cafe, catch the eye of anyone who is looking in your direction, nod at them, smile and move on to the barista to place your order. This simple interaction is the first step when you are introducing yourself in a social situation. It is completely non-verbal. However, this polite exchange allows you to exercise your ability to communicate even though it was non-verbal. One crazy and unique thing about shy people is that we usually tend to avoid contact with anyone else and just narrow in on our objective and get out as soon as our mission is accomplished.

You would have to retrain yourself and retrain your brain in the process. When you attend an event, instead of just getting in and getting out, allow yourself to experience what is going on. When the event is over, you can linger around for a few minutes and say hello to at least two or three people before leaving. These smaller interactions will provide positive memories for you to feed on as you start to take bolder steps towards your social goals. We will cover more of this in the next chapter but for now, make it your mission to build more positive social experiences no matter how small.

Chapter Eight

Effective Leadership for Extremely Shy People

Being a shy person in a leadership position can be a nightmare. This nightmare is even worse if this is something you did not work towards. That is because a lot of us just want to be able to do our jobs and move on. In the previous chapter, I talked about how most shy people tend to simply focus on their objectives, ignore everyone else and then retreat into their haven the minute the mission has been accomplished. This has to change if you are going to build strategic social alliances.

Setting Firm Boundaries

Shy people have a negative perception of a leadership position. They assume that it means you have to be bossy which is not the case. Leadership is about taking charge of a project and guiding your team towards a collective objective. It is as simple as that. So the first place you need to start with is changing your perception of what a leadership role is. When you understand who a true leader is, it makes it easier for you to assume that role.

In any situation, a leader is tasked with the responsibility of helping the group that he or she leads to reach a collective goal. This does not mean everyone has to like you or is that everyone has to hit you it doesn't mean that you have to suddenly stop being people's friends and also does not means you have to become the enemy either the only way to manage a leadership role effectively is by setting firm and clear boundaries this can be scary but it is certainly doable. Setting boundaries does not mean that the word "no" becomes your new favorite. It means that you have to help people on the stand what's their respective roles in very clear and concise terms.

To create a healthy environment for the group you lead to effectively manage their responsibilities, you need to be firm in establishing these boundaries. One way you can do that is by modeling it yourself. Through your actions, you can let people know what is expected and what will not be tolerated. You can't ask people to show up on time if you are coming in several hours late. You should also respect the boundaries that other people set. If the work time is allocated to a specific period, try to respect that. Pushing past that time frame can cause them to resent you. Also, ensure that the boundaries you set are not to power a personal objective or an excuse to continue in your introverted ways. The focus of these boundaries should be on the collective objective.

Voice Your Opinions

People cannot read your mind. I am sure that you know this already but for some reason you expect people to simply know what you want because of the environment you are in. As a leader, it is your responsibility to voice your opinions as long as they are related to the project at hand. Keeping quiet when you have ideas or need to call people to order is not going to do any service to the members of your team. It is scary to be the one who has to stand up and bring order when there is chaos but that is the job a leader is expected to carry out.

You don't have to shout or scream for your voice to be heard. The two things that are expected of you in both your actions and in your word are clarity and firmness. You should try as much as possible not to send mixed signals. Let your body language correspond with the tone of your voice and the message you are trying to pass across. Using penalties and harsh words will not make you an effective leader. It might get you some results but that will only take you so far. Firmness and clarity will help to provide a healthier work environment and when you have a healthy work environment, you naturally garner the respect of your colleagues and the people you are leading.

Sometimes, the people you are leading will be unfair to you and say critical things that hurt you. You must understand that this position is not about you. It is about the collective goal. Always happens at the back of your mind. If you feel hurt by what someone says, you can easily call them aside and let them know that you felt disrespected. If the person refuses to admit their wrongdoing and continues to say those hurtful things, then you can enforce the penalties for that action. This affirms your position as a leader and doesn't make you a mean person. Another thing to remember when you voice your opinion is to take into consideration the opinions and perspectives of other people involved. Being a leader doesn't mean your voice drowns out the voice of every other person. Instead, you are in a position where you ensure everyone's voice is heard and at the end of the day, the best decision that helps you and your team meet this collective goal is what is implemented.

Separate Work From Play

When you are in a leadership position, naturally, you would attract people who would want to get closer to you simply for the position that you occupy. There might also be genuine friendships that will be formed as a result of this. It is okay to be friends with these people especially if they are bringing value to you. However, as with the first segment in this chapter, you have to be clear in setting your boundaries. Conversations that happen outside the workplace should not be brought into play when you are at work and when you are outside of the workplace, try as much as possible not to bring your office personality into the situation.

As an introverted person, the sudden attention that your leadership position gets you might be very flattering and if care is not taken, it will cause you to make decisions that can compromise your position. Avoid this type of mess by separating work from play. In some instances, it will become necessary for you to cut back on communication with specific people if you feel that it makes it difficult for them to relate with you as a leader even when you are in a work environment. This doesn't make you mean or suddenly proud. It is part of the burden that a leader has to bear. You can try to explain it to them clearly so that they understand where you are coming from. But you must be firm in that regard.

One phrase I have used a lot in this chapter is "collective goal" and I am going to use it again here. Remind yourself over and over that this position is not about you. Yes, your skills and capabilities might have earned you that position but the people who put you there trust that you will be able to lead your group to where they expect you to get to and that should be your priority. Infusing play into work will blur out boundaries and reduce productivity. Even though you may feel as though people like you better for it, the fact is at the end of the day when productivity levels are low people will resent you for the same reason.

Master Your Emotions to Manage Your Team

An emotional leader is never going to be an effective one. Being an introvert means that you are extremely sensitive and react emotionally most of the time. In essence, being in a leadership position will contradict your true nature. But if you learn to discipline your emotions and work within the confines of your position, you stand a better chance of being an effective leader. An example of an emotional reaction is the situation where a colleague or someone on your team says something you perceive as insulting in front of everyone. Rather than breaking down, yelling, or retreating into your haven, your call of action should be to take them aside and let them know in clear terms how wrong they are for what has been said.

You cannot afford to be emotional as a leader. There are times when things will not go according to plan and there are times when you will experience abject failure. As introverts, our reaction when confronted with any of these scenarios is to retreat. But being a leader means you have to stand your ground and find the motivation to inspire your team to try again. For this to happen you need passion, not emotion. Passion is connecting your interests with what you are doing and allowing that to motivate you. When you are interested in something, you become invested and when you are invested, you become motivated. This will inspire passion and your passion will inspire those who follow you.

One thing I should say is that you should not fall into the trap of people who say, set your emotions aside. No. I disagree with that opinion. Your emotion can become a true motivation if you channel it correctly. Some of the greatest social changes in our society today happened as a result of emotions being channeled properly. What I am asking you to do here is to not react emotionally. Instead, through logical thinking and strategic action, you can convert those emotions that you feel, whether negative or positive into critical steps that will help you actualize the collective goals. When you can successfully do this, you will possess the makings of a great leader. So, the main message you should take away from this chapter is this; don't abandon your emotions but don't react to them either. Instead, channel it and harness it for the greater good of the people you lead.

Chapter Nine

Public Speaking for Novices

Once upon a time, standing on a podium with over a hundred pairs of eyes facing me was my worst nightmare. This was compounded by a negative experience I had in high school where I practically ripped the entire stage apart when I was called on to recite a poem. This memory was so deeply engraved in me that whenever I was told I had to speak in front of anyone no matter how small or loving the crowd was, I would go into some sort of crisis mode. My voice will turn hoarse. My knees would turn into jelly and I would be sweating profusely from every single pore on my skin until it looks like I am melting. Today, I have successfully overcome that fear and I want to share how I was able to do it. Because if I can go from that blubbering mess into the confident speaker that I am today, so can you.

Overcoming Stagefright

You know those horror movies where the door that offers escape for the victim suddenly seems as though it is miles away even when it's just a couple of feet away from there? I usually had this vision whenever I wanted to get on stage. In my mind, this stage would suddenly transform into this elevated platform that has all kinds of wirings and connections designed to ensure that I fell flat on my face and implode from shame. I think what I had was an extreme case of stage fright. But I overcame it and here are some of my tips that can help you do the same.

1. **Breathe**

    Take deep and calming breaths. This will help to regulate the heart rate and force you to focus on what is going on inside of you rather than the fear that the stage is inspiring.

2. **Redirect your thoughts**

    As your breathing regulates your heart rate and offers you a chance to think outside of your fears, direct your thoughts to those positive affirmations you have been working on about yourself and your ability to nail this speaking thing.

3. **Envision success**

    As you make your affirmations, create images of your success on stage. Picture yourself getting on there, delivering your speech, connecting with your audience, and having an all-around positive experience while you are there.

4. Be prepared

Sometimes the fear that you feel when you are about to get on stage is not because of some past experience. It could be a subconscious concern that you are not prepared enough. Eliminate that fear by being ready.

5. Just do it

Backing out every time you are presented with an opportunity to get on stage will only reinforce this pattern of behavior until it becomes a habit. No matter how scared you feel, put aside those fears and just do it.

Speech Development and Execution

This segment is in response to number four in the previous segment which encourages you to be prepared. When you are adequately prepared, you increase your chances of delivering an eloquent speech that will be appreciated by your audience thus, providing a positive experience for you to draw on. But what exactly goes into the preparation of a good speech for public speaking?

1. **Have a clear understanding of what you are expected to speak on**

   If you are expected to talk about human rights activism, let the focus of your entire speech be on this topic. Carry out as much research on the subject as possible. The internet is a great resource for this. Know the topic like the back of your hand. One of my favorite tips is to explore the topic I am asked to address in terms of the current social experiences. News articles and social commentaries are helpful in this regard. When you do this, you can help your audience connect the dots and this will help them relate better to what you have to say.

2. Understand your audience

Try to get information on the people you will be speaking to. If you are called in your workplace to speak, obviously you have a fair idea of the kind of people that are coming there. The next thing is to understand why they should be interested in what you have to say or why they would even want to listen to what you say. When you are equipped with the answers to these questions, you can create your speech in response to this and this will make it more effective at passing the message across.

3. Understand the organizers of the event

When you put your script against the backdrop of the people who have called you to make the speech, you align yourself with their goals, values, and objectives. This is important because, at the end of the day, you are not just speaking to the audience. You are also indirectly trying to sell the message of these organizers and the more aligned your message is with their mission, the better you will be at achieving this.

4. Use words that you are familiar with

By the time you get to this step, you have more than a fair understanding of what you want to say. This stage is about how you are going to say it. It is important to use words that you are familiar with so that you sound more natural. When you sound more natural, you will be more confident and at ease on stage. But if you try to use big words so that you sound intelligent, people will see through this facade and your insecurities will become even more evident. This will cause them to be distracted from the message. It is also important to speak in the language of your audience. If you are talking to semi-literate people, your language should fit in that category so that they understand what you are saying.

5. **Practice! Practice!! Practice!!!**

Now that you have completed the speech, the final step is to practice it as much as possible. I am not asking you to memorize your speech as this can backfire. Instead, what I am asking you to do is to internalize the message so that when you speak, you don't sound like a robot who is programmed with a message to deliver. You would sound more human-like. But because you are also familiar with what you are saying, you will sound like an expert on the subject. People naturally gravitate towards persons they perceive to know what they are talking about and practicing your speech will put you in that light.

Step into the Spotlight with Confidence

When you get on stage, you have to act confident even if you don't feel confident. This is a clear case of faking it until you make it and I don't see anything wrong with that here. The fact is that you are feeling terrified right now but you are also capable of getting on that stage and rocking your speech. What happens in between is determined by how confident you feel. Here are a few things that can help you build confidence before you get on stage and when you are on stage.

1. **Dress the part**

   I have talked about the power of body language. The way you dress is one of those subtle languages that communicate your essence even before you open your mouth. It doesn't have to be anything flamboyant or flashy but looking elegant and stylishly classic while ensuring that you are comfortable with what you are wearing can project a confident personality.

2. **Proper hygiene**

   No amount of perfume or body spray can mask body odor. You need to groom yourself properly so that when you wear your clothes, you can feel confident. Wearing clothes when you are not clean or properly groomed is like putting jewelry on a pig. It doesn't make sense. Plus, every time you walk past a person and they cringe as a result of the offensive whiff they get from you, your confidence will drop down a notch. Make sure you are properly groomed before you get on stage.

3. **Own the stage**

Stage actors have mastered the ability to make the most of the space they occupy when they get on it. No matter how big the stage is, an actor will figure out how to own it and make it appear as though they are larger than that space. When you speak, ensure that you project your voice so that people can hear you but don't scream into the microphone. When you move, ensure that you are pacing all over the place. Walk deliberately as if this is a path you often follow. As you walk and talk, alternate between hand gestures and facial expressions. All of these work towards making you seem like you belong on that stage.

Transparency with Your Fears

One of the many themes in this book has been about letting go of the illusion of perfection. Yes, I want you to be confident when you get on stage. Yes, I want you to sound like you know what you are talking about. Yes, I want you to step out of your shell and into the social light. But one thing I know that will probably never change is the fact that you are a little frightened by the prospect of doing these things. When you are on stage, the fear doesn't go away even if you have pushed through those mental barriers that kept you away from it and it is okay to own it when you get there.

Earlier on, I talked about this little trick I have when I am feeling a little bit too anxious or when I feel as though the fear is creeping in. I jokingly tell my audience how I feel. This usually elicits some sympathy from your audience and reduces the pressure to perform with perfection. Sometimes, I simply say things like, "if my hands start to shake or I suddenly trip off the stage, please note it is not because there is an alien force here. (I pause here because people laugh a little at this point). The truth is, I am frightened of standing in front of you but to overcome my fear I have chosen to be here and I hope this will serve as an inspiration to people who are also struggling with different types of fears and their lives". And then I make a transition to my prepared speech.

This speech allows me to be transparent about what I am going through. It can also serve as a teachable moment for the members of my audience. But most importantly, by confessing my true state of emotions, I take away that pressure and allow myself to truly enjoy my time on stage. Plus, if I trip or something, I can say, I told you so and laugh at myself.

Chapter Ten

Managing Short and Long Term Relationships

And finally, we are in the last chapter of the book. I feel like we have talked about a lot of things and that may seem like a lifetime ago. But we have finally come to the crux of everything. I am going to assume that you have already started implementing some of the things we have mentioned or that you have made notes on what you intend to do. This final step is about managing the relationships that you have as a result of taking those actions we have talked about.

How to Negotiate Any Deal

For anyone, negotiations can be tricky and uncomfortable. For a shy person, it is extra uncomfortable because you are required to do three things that go against your nature. One, you are expected to speak up. Two, you need to put sentiments and emotions aside to think logically and three, hold your ground while being flexible. Whether you are interviewing for a new job position or negotiating boundaries with loved ones, or bargaining with a trader at your local market, learning the art of negotiation and mastering it can ensure that you come out with an outcome that is beneficial to you.

1. **Establish a relationship**

   This is the number one rule for any negotiation is to establish some sort of rapport with the person you are negotiating with. Offer a sincere compliment. Make some positive comments about the situation or object you are bargaining over before you go in for the deal. Doing this will make your opponent more open to discussing your terms.

2. **Be sincere and open**

   I am not saying you should be overly trusting and pour out your entire life's history in the process. But make sure that whatever you say is sincere. So even if you are offering a compliment, let it be something that comes from your heart. Try to avoid making snarky remarks. This will immediately close off the person to considering your terms or even further negotiations.

3. **Voice your expectations**

   Whether you are buying a product or trying to nail that job interview, you must voice your expectations for the thing you are negotiating over. If it is a product, don't just focus on the price. Talk about your expectations. Ask questions if necessary. If it's for a job, don't focus on your salary. Talk about the work environment and other working conditions that you feel will make you more effective at your job. By exploring your expectations with the person, you force them to think not just in terms of costs now but in terms of what they have to offer to you. This will help to sweeten the deal and create a win-win situation.

4. Don't be afraid to walk away

People are not as dumb as you think they are. If you are negotiating over something that is of value to you, they can see it in your expression and mannerisms and can use it as leverage to get you to lean more towards their terms. No matter how precious an item is, try as much as possible not to be too obvious about your desire for it. Don't let your desperation show. There are very few exceptions to this rule but generally speaking, you should be able to give off the air that this is not the end of the line for you. Mentally speaking, this will put you and the person you're negotiating with on equal grounds.

Conversation Starters; Tips that Work Every Time

The biggest hurdle in any social situation is that opening line that introduces you into the conversation this is why pick up lines were born but you're not always going to try to pick someone up sometimes you just want to strike a genuine conversation so how do you go about it I'm not going to give you word for word the kind of conversation status to use but I'll offer you some tricks that can get you in the door.

1. **Sincerity**

    A simple hi or hello can be all you need to start a conversation if you are sincere in your expression. You can walk over to a group of people and say, "Hi I just wanted to come over and introduce myself in the hopes that we could have a small conversation". Some people will probably react negatively to this especially if the person you are trying to talk to is already engaged in a conversation with another person. But if you find them by themselves just like you, this could work.

2. **Common interest**

    Set us say you are a comic book fan and you find this person holding a copy of a comic that you are also interested in, you could use that as a segway to a conversation with them. Of course, the sincerity factor has to be at play here again because people can sense when you are just fishing for conversation as opposed to being genuinely interested in this thing you are trying to point out as a connector between the both of you.

3. **Asking for advice**

   If you are in a fashion store trying to buy an item and you see someone, maybe shopping for an outfit, it's okay to walk up to them and say, "Hi, excuse me. I hope this is not a bother but I was hoping you could tell me if this outfit compliments this other t-shirt". This is a nice and unpretentious way to get a conversation started in a non-formal way. In a more conservative setting, like in a networking event, you could ask the person's opinion on an article you read or something that was said at the event.

Becoming More Intentional About Your Actions

When you decide to become more social, you are given a clean slate to start over. I think you should be more deliberate about the choices that you make because, in this situation, you are not getting social simply because you want to have more friends and know more people. Yes, if this happens, it would be great. But you should be more selective about permitting the things that happen to you in this context. You shouldn't simply say yes to every event you are invited to. You should not allow toxic people into your space under the guise of making friends.

The fact is that you have had a lot of experiences that would probably justify your decision to avoid people completely. However, you have decided to do the opposite of what is expected and in doing so you must make a conscious effort to ensure that your mental and emotional happiness is protected at all costs. No friendship or relationship is worth the emotional and psychological trauma that toxicity in a person causes. Remind yourself constantly that you deserve happiness. You deserve the peace of mind. You deserve to be surrounded by people who accept you for who you are and uplift you at every opportunity.

As a shy person, one of your natural gifts is your ability to be remarkably loyal to the people you bring into your circle. So make sure that you pick those people carefully. That is not to say that the people you bring into your circle will not hurt you. I have learned in life that the people who hurt you are usually the ones you love the most. That being said, ensure that these people are not trapped in a cycle of bad behavior that constantly hurts those around them. Know that it is not your job to fix them. You can still learn to love them from afar. The point is to protect your mental space. Look for people who can contribute to building a healthy relationship that will allow those who are part of that relationship to thrive. When you have an inner circle that thrives, you as an individual will also thrive.

Arguments Have an Advantage in Relationships

Whether you are in a business relationship or a romantic relationship, whether it is a long-term situation or a short-term situation, as long as two or more people are involved, there is bound to be disagreement. Heck, even as an individual we have this internal mental battle between ourselves. When it comes to making decisions on certain things that conflict between your head and heart, you find yourself in disagreement... with yourself! This is a clear indication that not everyone in this world is meant to get along swimmingly well. However, the presence of argument as a result of those disagreements does not mean that your relationship is doomed to fail.

Having arguments and disagreements is an excellent opportunity for you to try out your conflict resolution abilities. It also helps you put your negotiation skills to the test. More importantly, it can allow both of you to get to know each other better. No matter how close you feel to a person, there will be situations where both of you will not be on the same page. There are some kinds of disagreements that can make you feel as if you people are from different planets. This probably explains the common description of men being from Mars and women being from Venus. It doesn't mean that men and women cannot get together and build a long-lasting relationship that is healthy and thriving. The problem lies in "how" the both of you argue.

When you express your disagreement in a way that demeans and belittles the other person, there is a problem. When a person constantly uses your differences in views as a basis to either break off the relationship or deny you simple rights in that relationship, there is a problem. For example, if your girlfriend or boyfriend says the relationship is over because you think Britney Spears is the greatest singer of all time as opposed to their Beyonce, then there is a problem. This speaks to immaturity and also points to the fact that the person in question is selfish. If you find yourself in any of these situations, you should voice out your perspective and get their reaction. If they fail to see this as a problem then it might be time to close that chapter and move on to something that will serve you better. It is not always easy but in the long run remember, you are all about being deliberate in the choices of people who you allow to get close to you.

Conclusion

First off, I think you should pat yourself on the back for making it through all 10 chapters of this book. I hope that you were able to learn new and important information about yourself. It is my sincere desire that the information I shared with you about my journey and my process will help you become more open when it comes to socializing. The ultimate message in this book is that being shy is not a problem or a limitation. Yes, being shy can make it a bit more difficult for you to get out there. But the moment you make up your mind to do so the doors will open up for you. If you can grasp this message, then I would consider my job done.

Before I go, I want to remind you that reading the book is not enough. Knowing the problem and the solution to the problem is not enough either. You need to take strategic steps. You must plot out an action plan which you will implement to enjoy the benefits of this book. Life will not automatically become sunny as a result. But I promise you, each day will become better. In moments where you met with people who are not entirely receptive, your confidence is not going to be bashed in. You will accept your refusal with grace, keep your head high and make your next move.

Also whatever you do, remember your affirmations. You are amazing. You are incredible. You are one of a kind and you are loved. It doesn't matter how many times you need to say it. The point is for you to hear it and internalize it. I see a lot of potential in you and I am super excited on your behalf about this next part of your life. With each step that you take, you get closer to the day when you feel more open and confident about living your dreams and doing life on your terms. You will forge amazing alliances, meet with incredible people and find the kind of friendship that will bring you the happiness you deserve. Thank you for allowing me to be a part of your journey. As you close this book, feel free to come back again whenever you need guidance or pointers. One day you will be the one sharing your story with the world. Until then, I wish you all the best.

Reference

Conquering Stage Fright | Anxiety and Depression Association of America, ADAA. (n.d.). Adaa.Org. Retrieved May 4, 2021, from https://adaa.org/understanding-anxiety/social-anxiety-disorder/treatment/conquering-stage-fright

D. (2017, January 16). The Art of Right Timing in Communication. Engaged Marriage. https://www.engagedmarriage.com/the-art-of-right-timing-in-communication/

George, C. (2021, April 19). 10 Ways To Step Out Of Your Comfort Zone And Overcome Your Fear. Lifehack. https://www.lifehack.org/articles/communication/10-ways-step-out-your-comfort-zone-and-enjoy-taking-risks.html

Henkel, J. K. (n.d.). How to set and maintain healthy boundaries as a leader. Biz Community. Retrieved May 4, 2021, from https://www.bizcommunity.com/Article/196/610/208456.html

Hsieh, C., & Hsieh, C. (2020, August 31). 10 Body-Language Signs to Brush Up on Before Your Next Zoom Date. Cosmopolitan. https://www.cosmopolitan.com/sex-love/a32599709/body-language-zoom-facetime-signs/

Keating, S. (n.d.). The science behind why some of us are shy. BBC Future. Retrieved May 4, 2021, from https://www.bbc.com/future/article/20190604-the-science-behind-why-some-of-us-are-shy

M., S. (2021, January 1). 7 Signs Someone Actually, Genuinely Likes You - P.S. I Love You. Medium. https://psiloveyou.xyz/signs-someone-likes-you-bd812d400226

Mamas, M. (2015, December 11). 5 Steps to Master the Art of Negotiation. Entrepreneur. https://www.entrepreneur.com/article/253074

Rana, H. (2020, May 31). 14 Things to Never Talk about on a First Date. She Began. https://shebegan.com/14-things-to-never-talk-about-on-a-first-date/

Tony, T. (2019, May 16). How to Overcome a Traumatic Experience or Event | Tony Robbins. Tonyrobbins.Com.

https://www.tonyrobbins.com/mind-meaning/reframing-traumatic-experiences/

Printed in Great Britain
by Amazon